LOURDES

by
David Baldwin

To Mary,
our loving Mother,
Queen of Peace,
our life, our sweetness and our hope

All booklets are published thanks to the
generous support of the members of the
Catholic Truth Society

CATHOLIC TRUTH SOCIETY
PUBLISHERS TO THE HOLY SEE

CONTENTS

Forword 3

Introduction 5

Lourdes - 1850s 7

Bernadette Soubirous...11

Our Lady of Lourdes 19

Sister Marie-Bernard...37

Saint Bernadette and the Messages of Lourdes.................55

The Lourdes Miracles 63

Lourdes and Pilgrimage Today...71

Select Bibliography 88

In having to bear their burden, many ask, *"Why?"*:

"Those who sow in tears," (*Ps* 126:5) 'in this world' (*Our Lady to Bernadette*)

"will reap with songs and shouts of joy" (*ibid*) 'in the other' (*ibid*).

FORWORD

The hundred and fiftieth anniversary of Lourdes will soon be upon us. The passage of time has meant much work has had to be done. The *Accueils* for the sick have been rebuilt. The Rosary Basilica is being completely restored, and work on the Basilica of the Immaculate Conception will follow suit.

But if stones grow older, Lourdes remains ever young. The Gospel message, in all its simplicity does not date. The natural features which play such an important role in Lourdes are universal and not constrained by time: water, the cave, the rocks and the light. Through the presence of so many of the sick and those who minister to them, through the diversity of languages and peoples, Lourdes has something to say to every person.

During the last few years, television broadcasts have featured Lourdes, and always in a favourable light even if the supernatural element has been obscured. Today, many young people - about the age of Bernadette herself - find peace here. Together with the sick and the handicapped, they form a second privileged group of Lourdes pilgrims.

Like many other pilgrimage destinations throughout the world, Lourdes remains popular. Yet those who come today often arrive as individuals or as members of informal small groups. With religious knowledge in general on the decline, it is necessary to give people of good will as much information as possible, and more importantly, help them enter into the profound reality of Lourdes.

This little book will help to further these objectives. Its modest size reassures the reader who wishes to quickly familiarise him or herself with the Lourdes; the place, the personalities, the events, the message and its history. There is no shortage of larger works available, should the reader wish to pursue his or her interests.

Be assured that the priests and helpers of the sanctuaries will give you a warm welcome.

✠ Jacques Perrier
Bishop of Tarbes and Lourdes
Feast of the Epiphany, 2004.

Introduction

Lourdes must be one of the better known towns in modern Christendom; a great number of Catholics all round the world must have heard of it and what the name stands for. The estimated six million pilgrims going there each year certainly endorse this as one of the most popular pilgrim destinations of the Christian world. Yet, before the apparitions of the Blessed Virgin Mary to Bernadette in 1858, Lourdes was just another small, nondescript provincial town tucked away at the foot of the Pyrénées in Southern France, struggling to seek a modern identity that would successfully lead it into the twentieth century. History would otherwise have passed it by - as it does any other small provincial town - unknown to all, save those who live in the local environs.

Similarly, Marie-Bernarde Soubirous, or Bernadette as she was known, was on the face of it, just another nondescript, small-town teenage girl in impoverished circumstance, seeking her identity in what she may have hoped would lead to many a young woman's expectations of the time - good health, a sound education, maybe a comfortable, loving marriage, maybe children. But her life, and that of the town, was to change dramatically during, and subsequent to, a five month period from February to July, 1858, when this simple, illiterate peasant girl of fourteen years was graced by God to receive His Mother, the Blessed Virgin Mary, in a series of eighteen apparitions.

This small book seeks to give a comprehensive account of the extraordinary events that brought the two together, earning one the crown of sainthood, and the other as being a place of Healing and Hope. It is then for the reader - in sensing any unanswered questions, or in being prompted to seek a way ahead through pilgrimage, or in yearning to fulfil a need - to decide on the next step. "Ask and you will receive, and so your joy will be complete" (*Jn* 16:24).

LOURDES - 1850S

The town of Lourdes sits in the lush, green, northern foothills of the Pyrénées. The hedonistic seaside resort of Biarritz is some 80 miles away to the West on the Atlantic coast. It is from this direction that the weather generally rolls in, with its variation of hanging, low clouds bringing damp and wet spells, to periods of peerless, scorching blue skies in the summer. The regional town of Tarbes, where the Diocesan Bishop resides, is some ten miles to the North, and the larger and better known spa town of Pau, is twenty five miles to the West. In administrative terms Lourdes was within the *département* of the Hautes-Pyrénées, being within the Bigorre region, with the indigenous population speaking, at that time Bigourdan, their own exclusive variation of Occitan (*langue d'oc*). Being a small, relatively isolated mountain community, and with its proximity to the Spanish border just over the Pyrénées twenty miles to the south, the inhabitants were probably very happy to play one national characteristic off against the other when it suited, particularly when attempting to maintain their own cultural identity in the face of creeping 'national standardisation'. A local historian specifically noted, "the inhabitants of Lourdes do not hold their beliefs cheap, and they do not abandon their grievances and their weapons quickly".

A typical small town

In the 1850s Lourdes had the status of a small town with a population of about 4,000. It previously held strategic importance in the Middle Ages, as confirmed by its eleventh century fortress still commanding the heights at the entrance of the Lavedan valley. A typical mix of small-town commercial activities, from the staging of local markets, to the fostering of an emergent tourist trade for those visiting the Pyrénées, as well as working marble and slate in the nearby quarries, was evident. But like many towns transiting the nineteenth century, its journey was being beset by a background of economic slumps, a decline in the traditional ways of earning a living and increasingly fierce competition in job markets, all hallmarks heralding the significant social and economic changes taking place in the early nineteenth century. Despite progress on these fronts, the area was still being affected by age-old scourges of pestilence periodically affecting the crops and giving poor harvests, and prevalent illness, chiefly in the form of tuberculosis and cholera. In 1854 these two afflictions of pestilence and disease conspired to give a particularly hard year in the Hautes-Pyrénées.

In terms of population there was quite a contrast: on the one hand there was a prosperous and educated section of the community, with a desire for learning and progress, and with the means to achieve this, as evidenced by the four schools and town newspaper; on the other, there was a disproportionately large, poor, peasant population, with their roots still firmly set in the traditional ways, with little access to regular, quality education or formal employment opportunities. This population contrast was also reflected by the mix of slum areas with the prosperous; medieval buildings with modern. The living quarters for the poor of Lourdes tended to the low lying areas of the old town prior to expansion and modernisation. There was, also, alongside the prosperous and the industrious, a reputation for violent crimes, noted as quite common in the mountain communities of those days. As reported in Therese Taylor's book, *'Bernadette of Lourdes'*, "Even women engaged in public brawls, and murders were committed in every day disputes, such as the sale of land or the theft of a sheep".

A darker side

The town also had a reputation for recalcitrance to outside authority, including the Church. For despite being, on the face of it, 'a desirable parish' with a reasonable standard of living and a large congregation, there was latent friction between the parishioners, determinedly fixed in their ways, and the priests who had to tolerate this. The local diocesan authorities, responsible for provision of parish priests reportedly came to "dread the very mention of its name". The people of Lourdes were the butt of regional humour, exemplified, for instance in badly prepared or cooked food being described as 'Lourdes cuisine'.

Whilst not specifically mentioned by name, there was a history - again as seemingly befits isolated communities - of witchcraft and sorcery in the local areas, and various witches were known in and around Lourdes, often sought out for their charms and cures. The last attempted witch burning in France was reported as being perpetrated in the Pyrenean community of Pujo in 1850, an event described as evidence of 'profound ignorance'. One particular folklore scholar of the time, Eugène Cordier, commented of the Pyrenean folk that he studied, that he looked forward to the day when, "legends, fictions, and all types of errors will leave the memory of the people, to forever be consigned to the grave domain of history". To the cultured these stories probably only added to the pastoral charm of the place, to the Bigourdanians they were very real and to be taken seriously.

It is against this background that this small isolated town, struggling with the times, would experience, through the action and reaction of two individuals, an upheaval that was to have consequences that at the time would have seemed incredible. The action was that initiated by The Blessed Virgin Mary, as God's messenger, appearing in Apparition in a riverside cave on the outskirts of the town; the reaction was that of an uneducated teenage peasant girl, Bernadette Soubirous, to whom Our Lady appeared, and on whose slender shoulders lay the responsibility for transmitting this event in a credible and consistent manner.

Bernadette Soubirous

Marie-Bernarde Soubirous was born in Lourdes on 7th January 1844. She was the first-born of parents, François and Louise. She was baptised two days later, soon acquiring the familiar name of Bernadette. At the time family circumstances were auspicious. Her parents were the de facto inheritors of her maternal grandparents' flour mill, Boly Mill, a successful and prosperous business. As the only child amongst adults she was loved and no doubt spoiled by the extended family that lived there, but unusually, whilst still a baby, she was put out to a wet nurse following an accident which prevented her mother being able to continue breast feeding. It was not until she was two that she returned home again to be greeted by her new baby sister, Marie-Antoinette (familiarly known as Toinette). By this time the extended family living at Boly Mill was in argument and disarray and in the process of going their separate ways, leaving, in 1848, Bernadette's parents with the prospect of running the mill without the advice, skilled help and motivation previously given by the close family.

Family difficulties

Bernadette's father, François, is described as being a peaceful and humble man, a good and reliable worker under an employer's supervision, but with little business acumen. These traits soon took their toll, and the business failed, ironically through their over-generosity, of which advantage was soon taken, and eventually lack of money to buy new machinery necessary to keep the business competitive. The Soubirous family were forced to move from the mill in 1854, under the cloud of debt and scorn. By this time their own family had grown, and of the nine children that the Soubirous were eventually to have, six had been born, of which the survivors were Bernadette, Toinette, their brother Jean-Marie, aged four, and a new born baby, Justin.

In a series of moves from one wretched lodging to another, and another failed business venture, the Soubirous finally ended up in the famine year of 1857 in the now celebrated *cachot,* the former prison cell, judged to be too unhygienic - even by nineteenth century standards - to be used for this purpose, and being underneath the house of one of Louise's cousins. In this stinking, cramped, vermin ridden cell, overlooking a cess pit and barely twelve feet by fourteen, the family of six took up residence with their meagre possessions, and continued the grim, unremitting grind for survival.

Despite these privations the family were generally remembered as being loving and affectionate, and Louise was described by one of her relatives as being, "a good Christian, kind natured and hard working. She brought up

her children well". However, probably in keeping with
the times, love was tempered by discipline and the cane,
as in a comment from one of Louise's sisters, "their
mother brought them up well, without sparing the rod;
and I also used a cane to keep my children in line". They
were also essentially a devout family, judging from
reports of neighbours that they could be heard saying
their prayers together every evening. There was,
however, a darker side, as François in particular had
gained the reputation of becoming a heavy drinker and a
bit of a layabout, and Louise was also reported as
succumbing to alcoholic bouts. These activities, should
be judged, though, within the strata of society in which
they now found themselves, where over-indulgence of
alcohol was seen as typical rather than outrageous.

So it was against these destitute and humiliating
circumstances that François and Louise sought what work
they could to support their family. François, blinded in
one eye in an accident at Boly Mill, found what casual
jobbing work that was available, although one of the
relatives commented that, "he did not exert himself for
every type of work". He also suffered the ignominy in
1857 of being branded a thief. He was suspected of
stealing a bag of flour, and then accused of the theft of a
plank of unexplained wood in his house. He was jailed
for a few days, but then released for lack of evidence to
prosecute. Nonetheless the 'mud stuck'. Louise worked in

laundries, laboured in the fields and scavenged for wood in the nearby forests. Set against this background of family deprivation and humiliation was economic depression, famine and disease in the area.

Childhood days

Reminiscences of Bernadette during this period give a picture of a 'dreamy and careless child', but also kind-natured and conscientious. Physically she was tiny, even by the standards of the short statured people of the region. She was seen as a resolute little person, gamely lugging her baby brother around on her hip, and her face was described as, "round and pretty with beautiful soft eyes". Certainly our own image from the pictures we see of her depict a reserved, calm person, seemingly always striking a slightly defensive pose with a challenging look, but one softened with liquid eyes, a neat nose and a soft, full mouth. She was clean, tidily dressed and neat, and despite her impoverishment, maintained a dignified way of conducting herself in an echo of how she would have done in better circumstances.

But even in better circumstances she would have been in poor health which the conditions of poverty only served to exacerbate. She developed asthma at an early age, but she did survive to adulthood five of her brothers and sisters, four who died in infancy, and her brother, Justin, dying aged 10. In Toinette's words, Bernadette, "had a bad chest, she ate very little". It says something for God's plan for her that against all the statistical odds for children of her age in that region, aged eleven, she survived cholera. But this left her even more weak and sickly; the violent purging had ruined her digestive system, and thereafter she had difficulty in digesting the staple foods of the region, often vomiting after eating. All her life she bore, and wore, the mantle of the sick, a sure presaging of the healing mission of Lourdes. In fact her philosophy on life in those days was summed up when she commented at a later stage, "When one desires nothing, one will always have what one needs".

The family's impoverished state made her the natural 'second mother' to tend the young ones whilst her mother was out working. She also worked as an occasional waitress. This undertaking of these familial duties in her earlier years effectively deprived her of any real chance of a sound education, and not only this, it also meant that her younger siblings, without family duties, went on to receive some form of education. Much evidence suggests that she was not an intelligent girl given to swift academic learning or retention of facts, she in fact had a poor memory.

This lack of formal education also had a knock-on effect in her spiritual life and development. Her family duties also kept her away from the catechism classes so vital to preparing for First Holy Communion, and her lack of general education meant that 'catch up' was virtually impossible. This first encounter with the Sacrament was seen as an important threshold to be crossed in a child's life - leading to acceptance into the adult world. Again Bernadette suffered the disappointment of seeing her younger sister, Toinette, going to the communion rail, while she looked on. What is certain though, through the words of her aunt, was that, "the rosary served as her school book". She would, of course, have known the common prayers of the day, so although lacking in formal religious education she certainly had experience of her Catholic practice, and particularly of the significance of Our Lady.

Away from home

In 1857 another ironic twist came to Bernadette's life. Madame Lagues, her former wet nurse, who had kept in touch with the Soubirous family, asked that Bernadette, now aged thirteen, came and lived and worked in her household in Bartres, an hour's walk from Lourdes. This was potentially a godsend to the Soubirous family having one less mouth to feed, particularly now that the other children were largely self-sufficient. In fact, the Soubirous offered the services of their other children too, but Mme Lagues specifically wanted Bernadette.

Bernadette's tasks at Bartres were looking after the five Lagues children, a job she was well equipped for, and tending the sheep, one which she was not, but it was not a particularly onerous one. It was during this short sojourn that many of the inaccurate depictions of Bernadette as mystic shepherdess grew; stories of her flock of sheep crossing the parted waters of a swollen stream, or not getting wet from the rain. Bernadette emphatically denied these stories, much to the disappointment of her admiring wishful thinkers. The reality of life at Bartres was one of austerity and harshness. For the Lagues were the very opposite to the Soubirous in the peasant milieu. They were frugal, hardworking, very pious, and with their family small-holding had reaped the benefits. Mme Lagues' attempts at teaching Bernadette the catechism ended in her frustration at the girl's lack of learning ability. There seemed to be an alternating display of love/hate for Bernadette; some witnesses describe her love for the child, others that she hated and mistreated her. In Bernadette's words, "my wet nurse was not always kind".

Simple spirituality

Although her mother had remarked that from a very early age Bernadette showed "a marked inclination towards piety" there was nothing particular during the Bartres period that seemed to mark her out for sainthood. On her deathbed Bernadette was asked whether she had recited the rosary in the fields at Bartres, "I don't remember that", she replied. She liked to construct little altars and shrines in May, but that was local practice and nothing unusual. Was she pious? "Oh! Like everyone else", was one of the Lagues girl's reply. But - there was undoubtedly something there, not as explicit and overt as the Fatima children, but something. It is summed up by René Laurentin as a, "spirituality hidden in simplicity... the holiness of Bernadette lay outside the bounds of any spiritual instruction... Bernadette was a stranger to all reflective awareness. She lived a spiritual night. To put it plainly and simply it was the night of the *pauvres,* the 'poor little ones' who awaited the Good News while carrying out the 'will of God' and enduring what he permits" (*Bernadette of Lourdes*), the last phrase a sentiment expressed by Bernadette herself at the time.

Bernadette herself instigated the end to her time at Bartres. She was determined to return to Lourdes to prepare herself for her First Holy Communion. She returned to the *cachot* early in 1858. Whilst the family was still no better off materially, she finally started receiving a regular education, and more importantly to her, formal instruction in catechism with Abbé Pomian, vicar of Lourdes. Whatever thoughts her parents, or Mme Lagues, had about Bernadette returning to Bartres after she had received her First Holy Communion can only be speculative, as the events which started on 11th February, two weeks after she had returned home, were dramatically to change the course of her life, that of her family's, and that of the small town of Lourdes.

Our Lady of Lourdes

Our Lady appears

Thursday, February 11th 1858 was the day Our Lady revealed herself to Bernadette in the grotto at Massabielle (Old Rock) by the river Gave just outside Lourdes. The grotto itself was not a particularly savoury place, full of river-swept debris and where pigs had been kept. Bernadette had gone there that morning with her sister and a friend to gather firewood and bones. They had gone on ahead, and whilst she was dithering about how to cross the river she recounts, "I began to take off my shoes and stockings. I had just removed the first stocking when I heard a noise something like a gust of wind". As she looked up at the grotto she saw a wild rosebush moving in a breeze, whilst all else round it was still. Then appeared 'a gentle light' within the grotto, in which stood a beautiful young girl in a welcoming gesture.

Although fearful, Bernadette felt no compunction to run away. She tried to make the sign of the Cross, and found she could not raise her hand to her forehead. "The vision made the sign of the Cross. Then I tried a second time and I could. As soon as I made the sign of the Cross the fearful shock I felt disappeared. I knelt down and said

my rosary in the presence of the beautiful lady".
Although Our Lady fingered the beads of her own rosary,
she did not move her lips. She then signalled Bernadette
to approach, "I did not dare", after which Our Lady
disappeared, "just like that".

Our Lady chose to appear to Bernadette, in that same
grotto, eighteen times between that first vision on
February 11th and July 16th, 1858. She appeared in three
distinct phases. Firstly, what are described as her three
'inaugurational' visions on 11th, 14th and 18th February,
followed immediately by a series of apparitions during
what has been called the Holy Fortnight, where during
this period except for two, separate missed days, she
appeared twelve times. Lastly, the 'confirmatory'
phase, of three separate occasions, well spread from
March 25th, the Feast of the Annunciation, to April 7th,
and finally, Friday 16th July 1858, on the Feast of Our
Lady of Carmel.

Early speculation

In a region where fairies, spirits and witches resonated
alongside the devoutly religious, such happenings as
initially and reluctantly reported by Bernadette, inevitably
started raising curiosity, speculation, ridicule and hope
amongst the varied strands of that mountain community.
On the family side, Bernadette's parents were dismayed
at her revelations: on that first day her mother took the

stick to Bernadette, insisting, "You didn't see anything but a white rock. I forbid you to go back there".

But, despite these strictures, and only after reluctant consent from her parents, Bernadette returned to the grotto three days later on Sunday 14th February, responding to the strong feeling of compulsion that would become so familiar to her over the period. She went with some young friends and took some holy water. The group started the rosary. Once again the Vision appeared, but only visible - as on all occasions - to Bernadette alone. During this apparition Bernadette sprinkled the holy water towards the apparition, challenging her, "'If you come from God, step forward'...but, the more I sprinkled the more she smiled, and I kept sprinkling until the bottle was empty". She also went into a state of ecstasy.

In these early stages the local clergy were indifferent to such reports, Father Peyramale, the parish priest, did no more than comment, "We must wait and see". Her Superior at school, Mother Ursule Fardes, was more cutting after the reports of the second apparition, "Have you finished with your carnival extravaganzas?"

Our Lady speaks

Support and help unexpectedly came to Bernadette for her third visit to the grotto on Thursday 18th February. Madame Millet, a prosperous person to be reckoned with in the town, determinedly took Bernadette under her wing in an effort to establish who the beautiful lady was. This went to the lengths of pen and paper being provided, which Bernadette proffered to Our Lady during the apparition. In speaking for the first time, Our Lady simply said, "It is not necessary that I write anything down". Then followed the words which would ring with Bernadette for the rest of her life, "I do not promise to make you happy in this world, but in the other". Lastly, came her own request to Bernadette, noted for the strikingly courteous way in which it was put, "Would you be kind enough to come here every day for fifteen days?". This request heralded the Holy Fortnight.

Bernadette obeys

Bernadette had no doubts in her mind that she should obey the white lady's gracious invitation to attend her at the grotto over the next fortnight. And it seemed that no obstacle was going to deter her from this mission. For after this third visit and invitation, Bernadette seemed transformed in energy and character, despite intimidation from the authorities, scepticism and ridicule from the church, curiosity or adulation from townsfolk, and latterly throughout the region. Even the initial prohibition put on by her parents was of little effect, and as her mother sadly told a friend, "She is not usually disobedient, but she told me that she felt herself pushed to go by something that she could not explain". This formerly shy, sickly, reticent, immature teenager, of little education and with only a basic knowledge of her faith, now, almost overnight, displayed a strong and visible sense of purpose and commitment, of which no obstacle was going to deter.

This insistence and attitude must have been enough to convince her parents and relations of her resolute intent, as, after no doubt perplexed discussion, it was reluctantly agreed that Bernadette would be allowed to visit the grotto daily. Over the next five days (19th - 23rd February) she experienced four more apparitions, the content of which - prayers and secrets - were known only to Bernadette.

Features of Apparition

Of the visible features that soon became evident during the apparitions, was the obvious signs of ecstasy and trance that Bernadette fell into as soon as Our Lady appeared. There are many eye witness reports of this, and although sentiment and romanticism can easily colour and overstate these impressions, the best witnesses that one can turn to are the arch sceptics, one of whom was a Jean-Baptiste Estrade, one of the town notables and intelligentsia, and Bernadette's uncle by marriage. When he went to the grotto to satisfy his curiosity he reported that he saw many, "common women kneeling in prayer. I could hardly repress a smile at the facile faith of these good Christians". It was however, a scorn that was swiftly dispersed, for as Bernadette knelt and went into trance, she was suddenly, "...no longer Bernadette... she was

Bernadette Soubirous as a young girl.

like an angel in prayer, reflecting in her features all of the glory of the heavens... We, positivists of the first rank, so proud until that moment, we knelt like children".

Other indications of her transformed and trance-like state was her insensitivity to physical stimuli, the most striking example being when she obviously felt no pain or incurred no physical damage when the flame from a candle that she was shielding during an apparition continually played over her bare hands. This phenomenon was objectively observed during the seventeenth apparition by one of the town doctors, Doctor Dozous, who examined her afterwards, "Not the slightest trace of burns".

Increasing effects

As that Holy Fortnight progressed so did events in and around the town, with actions and reactions taking on their own momentum, and they seemed to ebb and flow round Bernadette, who was the unwilling centre of attention and remained largely impassive to them. The most visible manifestation of the events was the growing numbers who soon started going to the grotto to witness the goings-on. Estimates of numbers vary widely, but indications are from the handful on 19th February, thirty on the 20th, building through three hundred and fifty on the 25th, to over sixteen hundred on the 2nd March, ending with estimates from eight to twenty thousand on the 4th March, the last day of the fortnight. With these increasing numbers grew increasing

rumour and speculation as to who was appearing and for
what purpose. Accounts of miracles and healings started
circulating, further fuelling expectation and speculation.

Bernadette stands firm

With all this, the civic authorities started becoming
concerned with the prospect of large gatherings, creating
at best, congestion and crowd control problems in the
town, to at worst, civic unrest giving rise to local political
de-stabilisation. On 21st February Police Commissioner
Dominique Jacomet sought timely pre-emption of these
issues by summoning Bernadette for interview. From the
written record of this interview it is obvious that Jacomet,
who was not a stereotypical authoritarian, and was in fact
remembered warmly by many as a man of 'exceptional
ability and integrity' who stayed with the people during
the cholera epidemic, was completely nonplussed by this
person whom he initially thought to be a simple child,
either suffering from delusions, or part of some
conspiracy or fraudulent money-making venture.

After a long period of intense questioning it was
becoming obvious that Bernadette was unshakeable in her
assertions. In his frustrations Jacomet could only end the
interview with threat and bluster, "I am quite willing to fix
things up between us, but on one condition. Admit that you
haven't seen anything". "Sir, I did see something. I cannot
say otherwise". In an admission of defeat on this point: "At

least promise me that you will not go back to the grotto any more. This is your last chance". "Sir, I promised to go there". "All right then, have it your way. I am going to get the policeman to take you to prison". Bernadette did not move. Happily for Jacomet any execution of this threat was forestalled by her father who came to take her home.

The eighth apparition on Wednesday 24th February saw Bernadette weeping bitterly, prostrating herself and kissing the ground in response to our Lady's second spoken message, "Penance! Penance! Penance! Pray to God for sinners. Go kiss the ground for the conversion of sinners."

The spring uncovered

But, of the apparitions during the Holy Fortnight that claimed most attention through Bernadette's actions, was that of the ninth on 25th February. On this occasion, instead of kneeling in rapt fixation and transformation, Bernadette was seen to be actively engaged in searching for something. She moved in and out of the grotto, sometimes on her knees. Finally, near the back, she bent and started scooping her hands in the wet, sticky mud. On the first three attempts she examined the contents in her hands and rejected them. On the fourth, reluctantly and with some repugnance, she drank at the contents of the muddy excavation. On looking up, the crowd could see her face smeared with mud. She then picked and ate a few leaves of golden saxifrage that was growing nearby.

These actions caused great consternation and puzzlement amongst the crowd. For those who believed, or had been convinced that something Divine was present at the apparitions, like M. Estrade, it was a moment of embarrassment and doubt as to what these bizarre and grotesque actions were all about. For those who were scoffing anyway, this was simply proof, in the words of one, "She's mad!". Bernadette completed this episode by going back to her usual place to pray before leaving, unmoved by those jeers of some of the onlookers.

When asked why she did this Bernadette simply explained that she was told, "'Go and drink at the spring and wash yourself in it.' Not seeing any water I went to the Gave. But she indicated with her finger that I should go under the rock. I found a little water, more like mud, so little that I could scarcely cup it in my hand. Three times I threw it away, it was so dirty. On the fourth try I managed to drink it". That afternoon some of the towns folk returned to the grotto, and on seeing that a sizeable puddle had formed, scooped a bit more, eventually producing clear flowing water. From those days the springs have consistently produced nearly 27,000 gallons per day. And from those bizarre scrapings in the mud came the clear meaning, Lourdes was blessed with not just a holy spring, but one uncovered directly at Our Lady's bidding.

The civic authorities sought to up the tempo of prohibition through the *Procureur Impérial,* M. Dutour, summoning Bernadette to interview on the evening of the 25th of February. Dutour was seemingly contemptuous of "these miserable people, their language, above all their standards", who inspired, "not only doubt but also disgust". But despite his lofty attitude, he also came off second-best. Bernadette's replies were brief and cold, "I expect no profits in this life", and her demeanour won the grudging admiration of the *Procureur,* particularly when she spoke of "uncommon thoughts". By his own admission the only way he could stop her was by imprisonment, but as there was no evidence of any serious law breaking, including fraud, it would be difficult to justify.

The tenth and eleventh apparitions manifested the same words and actions from Our Lady and Bernadette of the eighth, invoking prayer and penance. The twelfth, on Monday 1st March, was 'silent'.

Church's reaction

The local Church authorities were becoming concerned for different reasons. Not only is the Catholic Church in general rightly extremely circumspect about reports of such happenings, but more so in this region of folklore and fairy tale. Of the many hundreds of apparition experiences reported throughout the world, very few even get to the point of being officially examined by the Church: it is a thorough, painstaking process described in detail in the CTS booklet *'Medjugorje'.* Father

Peyramale's early reaction of 'wait and see' was therefore
expected and typical, as was his prohibition on any clergy
going to the grotto. A certain Father Desirat, though, from
outside Lourdes and unaware of this, was present at the
apparition on the 1st of March. He watched Bernadette
with 'meticulous attention', "What a difference there was
between the girl she was then and the girl I saw at the
moment of apparition! ...the most consummate actor could
never reproduce her charm and grace".

However, the local clergy's difficulties soon
compounded in a very short space of time. The first was to
test Father Peyramale's tolerance to the limit, for during
the apparitions of the 2nd and 3rd March Our Lady instructed
Bernadette to, "Go and tell the priests that people are to
come here in procession and to build a chapel here". The
mere fact that Bernadette had the temerity to go to him
with these seemingly outrageous requests suggests some
superhuman courage and motivation on her part - for the
priest, although by now struggling with favourable images
of religious resurgence among his flock - Mass attendance
and confessions had gone up - was, nonetheless, not
impressed. He is described as angrily retorting, "...*you* can
go and make the procession; everyone would follow you,
you have no need of priests", and cutting off the second
vital part of the message about building the chapel.
Bernadette had to summon up yet more courage, and
bolstered by a friend's presence, returned to the presbytery,

with no doubt great trepidation, to relay the full message. His only tactic was that of obfuscation and delay - he demanded to know more about the Lady.

First miracles

The second difficulty that the parish priests had to contend with were the inevitable wildfire tales of miracles and cures beginning to occur as a result of grotto visits. Many were indeed just false rumour or wishful thinking, and efforts were made early on to trace and investigate such reports, either to debunk or support. Some indeed did prove to be miraculous, and emanated from those early days in the Holy Fortnight. Subsequently they underwent the proper investigations and were accepted by the Church as miraculous. Of these was a Catherine Latapie whose paralysed arm, with which she could neither cook or sew, was completely cured after bathing them in the grotto spring on 1st of March, as was the eyesight restored to stonemason Louis Bouriette, who was blinded in one eye in a mine explosion.

Holy fortnight ends

The day of the last of the fortnightly apparitions (4th March) dawned to a huge crowd gathered on both sides of the Gave, also a crowd with huge expectations. People had been there, praying, since 11pm the night before. The Police Commissioner diligently inspected the nooks and crannies around the grotto to forestall any mechanical or illuminatory trickery. Bernadette took her usual spot. She went into ecstasy on the second decade of the rosary. After about half an hour she went on under the grotto roof where she usually conversed with Our Lady. She was there for some short minutes, showing some sadness, some joy. After which she returned to her kneeling place and continued with the rosary for another quarter of an hour. After that, without saying a word, she snuffed out the candle and left for her home, oblivious to the vociferous and passionate questioning of the throng. There had been no miracle, no message, no revelations - it all seemed a huge and disappointing anti-climax.

She was besieged at her home that day by the faithful and the curious, something she endured with fortitude and patience, pointedly refusing to accept money or any form of gift. Despite these attentions she managed to find time to report back to the priest: "No, she gave no name, ...but she still wants the chapel." "Do you have the money to build this chapel?" "No, Reverend Father." "Neither do I, tell the lady to give it to you." Despite the lack of drama, it appears that many were satisfied with the sheer occasion of the day. The police were certainly happy as there had been no civil disorder. As noted by M. Estrade, "An opinion, so strongly held as to be a certainty... was that the Lady of the Grotto had not yet said her last word". Indeed she had not:

there was no mention of her having said farewell to Bernadette at that last meeting.

The relief of the civic and Church authorities, however, proved to be short-lived. Bernadette attempted to resume her normal life eschewing any personal attention. Her very telling response to those who sought her out for healing was, "I am not responsible for curing people, go and wash in the water of the grotto", presaging the future purpose of the holy spring that Our Lady bid be uncovered. And that is where people went, to the grotto, and that was what worried the authorities. People prayed there, candles were ever present, as were flowers, and a steady trickle of gifts and money were left. There was an air of hope and anticipation at Lourdes.

'I am the Immaculate Conception'

On 25th March, the Feast of the Annunciation, Bernadette once again experienced the irresistible urge to answer Our Lady's summons to the grotto. To her great joy Our Lady appeared, and after having said the rosary, Bernadette braced herself to pursue her visitor's identity. "Mademoiselle, would you be so kind as to tell me who you are, if you please?" At the fourth asking Our Lady ceased her smiling, extended her hands and raised her eyes, saying in the local patois with which she habitually addressed Bernadette, "*Que soy era Immaculada Councepciou* (I am the Immaculate Conception)". On completion Bernadette hurried straight to the presbytery, accompanied by her aunt, repeating these strange 'grown-up' words over and over again for fear of forgetting or getting them wrong.

Father Peyramale was astounded. "A woman cannot have that name! You are mistaken! Do you not know what that means?" Bernadette shook her head. "Then how can you say the words if you did not understand them?" "I kept repeating them along the way". One of Father Peyramale's first actions after this was to check with the Sunday school mistress that she had not mentioned the Immaculate Conception to her class. Realisation started sinking into his mind. Never before had Bernadette identified the apparitions specifically with Our Lady - in fact up to now she had always called it *'Aquero'* ('that'); it was others that had started the assumption, but Bernadette, as many children may have been tempted in seeking favour or affirmation, never endorsed it. In a way, the priest started feeling a great sense of relief as he reported all this to his Bishop by letter, because these were the words which summed up the dogma pronounced four years earlier by Pope Pius IX that Mary was immaculately conceived, 'preserved immune from all stain of original sin'. In appearing at Lourdes, Our Lady was simply confirming the reality of her status, and affirming what in fact the faithful were already believing in their hearts (*sensus fidelium*).

Final appearances

The penultimate vision was on Easter Wednesday, April 7th, where Bernadette quietly prayed in ecstasy with the Virgin. It was around this period that activities in, and associated with, the grotto seemingly started getting out of hand in the eyes of the authorities. Plans to have Bernadette hospitalised were thwarted by the doctors who themselves commented, "Is there any need to treat this affliction?" and that there was no danger to her health. There were reports of other visionaries and goings-on. The grotto was shut off, being declared as an illegal place of worship - which was largely ignored. In the words of René Laurentin in his book *'Bernadette of Lourdes'*, "The pure prayer of the apparitions period degenerated into pretence and superstitious, feverish rites". The greatest consolation and joy to Bernadette during this time was when she made her first Holy Communion on June 3rd, the Feast of Corpus Christi.

The solution to these problems, however, were remarkable in their simplicity: the Bishop of Tarbes, whilst still remaining neutral about the apparitions, officially denounced all these other goings-on in and around the grotto on 11th of July, and, "they disappeared in the twinkling of an eye". Later, the civic authorities, having to reckon with the reality of the situation, and on orders direct from Napoleon III, removed all the trappings of confrontation from the grotto, and in doing so all the confrontation and aggravation disappeared. Life at the grotto took on the air of pilgrimage, prayer and healing that has gone on to this day.

The final appearance of Our Lady to Bernadette, the eighteenth, happened on 16th of July, the Feast of Our Lady of Mount Carmel, in the evening at about 7pm. Direct access to the grotto was still at that time being denied by barricades; Bernadette knelt opposite the Grotto, on the other side of the river. It was again a low key and silent affair for onlookers. She went into ecstasy as she started the rosary, clearly joyous at seeing Our Blessed Lady, saying that, "she was more beautiful than ever". On completion she stood up - it was over. Her only comment on the way home was, "I saw neither the barriers nor the Gave. It seemed to me that I was in the grotto, no more distant than the other times. I saw only the Holy Virgin".

Our Lady's visits to Lourdes, initially heralded by nothing more than a stirring breeze, were gentle, almost prosaic, and to start with enigmatic, as if she were almost reluctant to immediately reveal her identity and purpose. It was only when she declared, towards the end of her visits, that she was the Immaculate Conception that everything suddenly and clearly fell into place, and that the message and mission of Lourdes, discussed in a later chapter, started impacting on the local people, and the local clergy, and rippling swiftly to the rest of the world.

SISTER MARIE-BERNARD

Bernadette, having moved in that short space of time from anonymous peasant girl to visionary of the Blessed Virgin, found herself being elevated on a local, regional and even national basis to that of celebrity. It was a situation that appalled her. The *cachot* was regularly being plagued by the curious from as far away as England, and they came from all strata of society, for the many purposes of satisfying curiosity, seeking cures, or vicariously basking in her reflected reputation. Many religious and priests came, including two local bishops who reported back to the diocesan bishop, Laurence, Bishop of Tarbes, and through their own conviction persuaded him to take positive action over the affair. The bishop responded swiftly, not only from his own spiritual discernment, but, "to respond to a public need, cure uncertainties and calm spirits". On 22nd July 1858 he published an Episcopal Ordinance to set up a commission of enquiry into the alleged apparitions. Its brief was to look into four specific aspects: the reported cures, the apparitions, the requests of the apparition, the origin of the Grotto spring.

Immediate aftermath

In dealing with her unwanted visitors, Bernadette continued to apply her minimalist approach, directly and briefly answering the question, but never elaborating. Her stock reply to those who continually challenged her over whether she had seen the Blessed Virgin was that it was her duty to tell the facts, but not to persuade people to believe in them. Her only moments of visible irritation, even anger at times, was when she was offered gifts or money - these were always brusquely turned away. When one reflects on the enormous responsibility that lay on Bernadette's physically and intellectually frail shoulders for maintaining a consistent and simple truth in the face of hours of sometimes hostile interview, one recognises a certain God-given charism of fidelity and fortitude within her - after all, it could have gone horribly wrong if she had succumbed to the temptation of the other route open to her: to espouse fame and undoubted fortune.

In this period immediately after the Apparitions, Bernadette again picked up some form of schooling through individual tuition, as well as working for nearly a year in 1859 as a nursery maid to an army officer's wife in the Lourdes garrison. However, she was always under pressure to carry on with formal education through boarding at the school/hospice run in Lourdes by the Sisters of Nevers. Initially, she resisted, not wanting to be separated from her family. The fortunes of the Soubirous family had also started to pick up, with François now in regular employment, and with the wages of two daughters, he could now afford to take a loan and return to his old trade as a miller in the Moulin Gras in late 1858.

But again their inherent over-generosity and irresponsibility as business people started to threaten this initiative. This potential demise, however, had a curious by-product. In exchange for offering up Bernadette to board with the Sisters, François took up regular employment with the local church, affording him a reasonable and steady income. Eventually, to further stabilise the situation the Bishop of Tarbes purchased a mill into which the family moved and paid rent. Bernadette was aware of this financial underpinning by the Church, and was grateful that it pre-empted yet another family humiliation and downfall; she acknowledged that as she was now tied to the Church by her bonds of holy obligation, so was her family, by bonds of debt.

On 17th November 1858 the Bishop's commission came to Lourdes to see the Grotto, talk to local witnesses and to Bernadette. In taking their evidence they were impressed by her calm demeanour and her lack of concern as to the status and number of her questioners.

Return to school

In July 1860, at sixteen years old, when other children her age had finished their education, Bernadette moved to the convent in Lourdes to effectively start hers as a boarder and pupil in the hospice. She was to stay there six years. In many aspects it was not easy for her. With years of erratic and minimal schooling she found the intellectual effort of formal learning very taxing; she was continually suffering from her asthma attacks - twice during this period as to cause concern over her life; she was subjected to endless visits by those many people eager to hear her story. The last two seemed linked, as recounted by the Sister who nursed her, "The long interrogations annoyed her... she would then have asthma attacks; we had to carry her to bed; she never blamed the visitors". Even the sick bed was not necessarily a respite, as visitors were often brought to her there. She had to endure the novel experience, for those days, of being photographed; she hated the thought of her image being treated as a commercial object, commenting at one point when she was asked if she was proud of this, "I do not have any basis to be proud, I have seen myself in the shop window of Lourdes on sale for ten centimes". At one stage, she was ordered to show herself in order to pacify a crowd which had gathered outside the hospice; she protested, "You are showing me off like a strange beast".

She was of course under intense and close scrutiny most of the time, which must have imposed its own burdens and pressures for someone already under expectation to behave like a saint. She has been described as variously stubborn on the odd occasion, and mischievous and 'prankish' on others. She sought to own nothing, and her abhorrence of money or gifts only grew stronger. Her piety was described as "ordinary but irreproachable", and that she "maintained a level of unostentatious devotion", keeping her rosary always in her possession, and reciting it at any free moment. She showed more aptitude, and got more satisfaction, from her embroidery skills than academia. Intriguingly she took up snuff, believed in those days to be an antidote against asthma, and which gave rise to one of her pranks induceing gales of powerful sneezes through giving her classmates snuff!

Bishop's decision

On 18th January 1862, after three years of deliberation by the Diocesan Bishop's commission of enquiry, the Bishop pronounced his decision as the Ordinary of the place, "We judge that MARY IMMACULATE, MOTHER OF GOD, really did appear to Bernadette Soubirous, on eighteen occasions from 11th February 1858 at the Grotto of Massabielle, near the town of Lourdes; that these Apparitions bear the characteristics of truth; that the faithful can believe them as true. We humbly submit our judgement to the judgement of the Sovereign Pontiff, who is responsible for governing the Universal Church". This simple, short statement opened the way for the legitimising and facilitating of veneration to Our Lady in Lourdes, formally celebrated on her Feast day on 11th February. By this recognition, Bernadette hoped that attention would now be taken off her, and allow her to live a 'normal' life, in whatever form that might take.

In the winter of 1864 she showed great tenderness and skill when she was given the task of tending a badly burned, bedridden old woman in the hospice. This experience reportedly had a great effect on her according to Father Pomian her confessor, "She tried her hand at caring for a couple of old people... fairly disgusting ones. She applied herself to the work with charity and developed a taste for it". Again one cannot help but think that this example and action was a strong portent of the future role of the Sanctuary at Lourdes.

The future

As her time went on in the hospice, questions about her future, and whether this included a religious vocation, inevitably kept coming to the fore. Bernadette never seemed to have any serious doubts about her desire for a religious life, but assumed that her health and intellect were an obstacle, as was her poverty, in the days when women entering convents were expected to provide a dowry. These concerns were confronted by Bishop Forcade of Nevers, when he visited Lourdes in September 1863, and reassured her that her worries were not valid. "Well, in that case, I'll think about it; but I haven't really decided yet". With these thoughts over the next months came solicitations from various convents and orders throughout France, and in finally coming to her decision in April 1864 one major factor in her deciding to go to the Sisters at Nevers was undoubtedly, "I am going to Nevers because they did not lure me there".

In fact that decision now prompted doubt and worry from the Superior General of the Order, Mother Joséphine Imbert, that Bernadette's 'celebrity status' would upset the equilibrium of the religious house. But with the support of the Bishop and the Mistress Novice the decision to accept her was taken in November 1864. However, her entry to the convent was delayed by three events: a relapse in her health, the death of her brother Justin, aged ten, and the requirement by the Bishop of Tarbes that she attend the inauguration ceremony of the Crypt, being built over the Grotto, on 19th May 1866. This she did, taking part in the first official procession in response to our Lady's request.

Departure

The time for departure finally came, and after having said a sad farewell to that familiar and special place where she met Our Lady, "The Grotto, that was my heaven", and her family, she left Lourdes never to return, arriving at the Convent of the Sisters in Nevers, on 7th July 1866 to take up her vocation in the religious life. Whilst not articulated by her at the time, the realisation must nevertheless have been there, as, later on in her life she reflected on the enormity of this move, "It is finished. Never again in my life will I see Lourdes". For this move was not only physical and geographical, it was also social and cultural, as Bernadette was now moving into a completely different milieu altogether, not only to a religious house far away from Lourdes, but to an Order that only accepted entrants from families of 'good standing'. This implied well-off families who could provide not only a generous dowry and trousseau, but who could also pay board and lodging during their novitiate, whereas Bernadette would be joining from a different stratum of society and on the basis of charity. It was also a move that would separate her from her own family for good.

Sister Marie-Bernard

Bernadette, soon to be professed as Sister Marie-Bernard, spent nearly thirteen years - and what was to be the rest of her life - at the Convent in Nevers, the Mother House of the Sisters of Charity. In all aspects, her life was a roller coaster of highs and lows. By her own words and desire she had come to Nevers "to hide herself". Her community had the same sentiment in mind, but throughout there remained an ambivalence to this. There was a struggle to acknowledge that whilst Bernadette was no ordinary nun, and although efforts were made to try and treat her as such, exceptions always seemed to arise. As a community, and as individuals according to their station within it, they also had to cope with the innate and understandable feelings of curiosity and awe in having such a person in their midst, as well as cope with that subconscious glow of pride that she had chosen to come and live in their community.

She had to become very wary, even at that stage, of those who were unashamedly 'relic hunting', for instance asking her to handle their rosary or other items. Regrettably, senior clerics were not immune from this, as in the account of a Bishop visiting her in her sick bed, who pointedly left his cap on her bed, expecting and hoping that she would pick it up for him. When it was obvious that she would not, he was forced to ask her to do it, at which she very politely replied, "Monseigneur, I did not ask you for your cap, you dropped it, now you can pick it up".

Personal struggles

These struggles in personal relationships with Bernadette were reflected in many different ways; Mother Joséphine Imbert, the Superior General, made a point of eschewing any signs of favouritism by adopting a cool and distant attitude towards her. The Novice Mistress, Mother Marie-Thérèse Vauzou, treated Bernadette severely, making it clear to her that her novitiate was going to be a period of testing, illustrated by her remark, "We are not worthy to have her, but one must do violence to heaven". One must also recognise the austere and disciplined approach applied to anyone undergoing formation in religious life in those days, and the concern, in Bernadette's case, particularly for those in authority, that they were seen not to display any sign of misplaced veneration for 'an ordinary nun'.

There was also the desire to ensure, again especially in Bernadette's case, to keep her humble; in the words of Mother Vauzou, "God deigned to let Mother Joséphine Imbert and me to be severe to Sister Marie-Bernard in order to keep her in the ways of humility". And as ever, she continued to live under close scrutiny all the time, maybe not the open-mouthed curiosity shown outside the community, but one probably far more critical and subtle, as commented on by one of her fellow Sisters, "They always had an eye on her and I believe they were more severe in noticing, in her, things which would have been let pass in another".

Visitors

On the day after she joined the convent Bernadette was required to address some 300 nuns and give her account of the Apparitions. This was presumably an attempt to forestall any future curiosity or speculation by the members of the community, but in effect, this probably only served to emphasise right from the beginning that she was unavoidably 'someone special'. And this continued throughout her convent life, that she would, in comparison to all her fellow sisters, be different, in that visiting prelates, bishops, benefactors and official historians of the church insisted on calling at the convent

Pilgrims gather before the Basilica - Lourdes.

explicitly to visit her. "How odd that a bishop should put himself to the trouble of hearing the Confessions of sick Sisters", was a remark she made, one not without irony.

Although having an understanding of, and an obedience to receiving these visits, they nonetheless irked her, to the extent on one occasion she cried out, "You promised me!", when confronted with the prospect of another visitor. On occasions, incidents were sometimes contrived to bring the visitor, seemingly by coincidence, in contact with Bernadette, which at times Bernadette would mischievously seek to frustrate. One marvellous example of this, demonstrating not only Bernadette's impish sense of humour, but how truth can take many forms, was when a woman who came in to the convent enquired of her, not knowing her identity, if she might see Bernadette. Bernadette replied, "Certainly Madame, watch that door, she will be going through it", at which she promptly went through, never to be seen again by that erstwhile visitor!

The visits that probably caused her the most distress, literally so, to the extent that they continued remorselessly into her final illness, was that of competing historians, keen to extract every detail of her experiences, which gave forth the anguished remark, "All those things... are already so far back, so long ago. I no longer remember. I do not like to talk about them too much because, my God, what if I made a mistake!".

Health

The other major visible factor of her life was her health. Throughout those years it was up and down, sometimes robust enough for her to contribute to the daily practical work of the community - from 1867 to 1874 she worked in the infirmary and the sacristy - on others there were many periods of infirmity and relapses with her acute asthma and fragile digestive system. Her peak period of good health was between 1870-72, but before and after this period she had many serious alarms, receiving the Anointing of the Sick at least three times, and on one occasion, in the early days, received Extreme Unction, and had to make a (premature) death bed profession of her religious vows to the hurriedly summoned bishop, as she was not expected to last the night (25th October 1866).

Profession and assignment

On 30th October 1867 Bernadette, with 43 other novices, formally made her religious profession with Bishop Forcade, who had supported her entry into the Order, officiating. Those professed Sisters were then assigned their initial tasks within the Order, all of which involved dispersion to the other 260 Houses of the Order throughout France. Again exception had to be made for Bernadette in the effort to protect her privacy. She had to be retained and assigned a job in the Mother House, but without the impression of favouritism, as jobs here were regarded as 'the cream' within the Congregation. In contriving this the Superior General said to the Bishop, "We could keep her here out of charity and give her some sort of work in the infirmary, even if it be only to clean up and prepare beverages for the sick. Since she is always ill, it would be right up her street". The Bishop agreed to this, and then added to her, "I give you the job of prayer".

Sorrows and joys

Other milestones in her life at the Convent were the death of her mother, Louise, on 8th December 1866, aged 41 years, of which most was spent in hardship and poverty, and having given birth to nine children, of which only four survived her own death. In February 1871 her niece by her beloved sister Toinette died, aged four. On 4th March 1871, her father, François, died after a short illness on the anniversary of the last Apparition of the Holy Fortnight. He had been planning to visit Bernadette for the first time later that year. Later in that March her aunt Lucile died, followed in August by Toinette's son, Bernard Sabathe, dying aged one. In writing to her sister, she displayed her submission to God's will: "But let us always remain subject, however greatly afflicted, to the paternal hand that is striking us so hard lately. Let us bear and embrace the cross".

With the lows of illness and sadness there were also moments of gaiety and laughter, and her mischievous nature would sometimes get the better of her. On being rebuked by the Sister who worked in the kitchens for taking water from a tap without being instructed and told to put it back, only provoked an outburst of laughter from Bernadette, who had visions of trying to get the water back in the tap. This completely disarmed the normally severe cook, who observed, "There was that little snip of a nun laughing. A bigger one would have bawled her eyes out". Bernadette obviously had skills as a mimic, as reported by one of the Sisters on her imitations of the convent doctor, Robert Saint-Cyr, "...Bernadette diverted us to the point of tears in imitating him, with a lively spirit and even a touch of malice. But the bounds of charity were always respected".

Other first hand glimpses of Bernadette come from other sources such as Doctor Saint-Cyr when he wrote, "An infirmarian who fulfils her task to perfection. Small and puny, she is 27 years old. She has a calm and gentle nature. She takes care of her sick patients with a great deal of intelligence... She also exercises great authority and has my full confidence". On occasions she was also observed exercising a sharp tongue, but invariably in situations where in, "acts for which she was reproached as impatient or sharp, it was rather the sentiment of justice which motivated her". The final note from the Novice Mistress, Mother Vauzou, summed her up as, "a stiff character, very irritable; modest, pious, devout, she is very orderly".

"The job of sickness"

From 1875 the occasions and length of her remissions from her sickness decreased, and the rest of her life truly started to take on, as she describes it, "The job of sickness", declaring also that it was the only thing that she would ever be good at. During much of this period she was confined to her bed, her "little white chapel" as she called it. Occasionally, a partial remission would allow her to get up and about, like in the summer of 1877, when she noted in correspondence, "I take a walk in the garden every day to restore my strength". From these correspondences and her conversations she always remained positive, talking optimistically about the future. However, any such optimism only served to disguise her worsening condition. At times she could not keep food down for long periods, was spitting blood, she had distressing asthma attacks, and tuberculosis was insidiously starting to eat away her bones, manifested particularly by an agonisingly ulcerated knee.

During the latter part of this period it was also evident, although Bernadette made very little specific reference to it, that she was suffering some form of spiritual torment, as evidenced by her tears on one occasion, and her reply to her fellow Sister's concern, "Oh no! It's not that [I am sick] ...if you knew all that was going on inside me... Pray for me", and on another occasion, "It is truly painful not to be able to breathe, but it is even more painful to be tortured by interior pains. That is terrible". The most specific indication that we have as to the source of this suffering was the remark made by her confessor, Father Febvre, "She often reproached herself for not having 'paid back' God for all the graces she had received".

Final days

On 22nd September 1878 she made her perpetual vows, following which, in December, she was confined to bed, only occasionally getting up to sit in an armchair. Her condition is graphically described by Father Cros, "Ankylosis of the knee... terrible pain: a huge knee, impaired leg, which one hardly knew how to move. Sometimes it took an hour to change her position. Her facial expression changed greatly: she became like a corpse. She who was very energetic in her desire for suffering, was completely vanquished by the pain". One of the Sisters who sat with her during one night recalls the torment that she witnessed, "One by one I heard the hours sound, and when the chimes ceased the same sighs continued... That is how I passed that terrible night, like someone at the foot of a living crucifix".

On 28th March 1879, seeming close to death, she received Extreme Unction, after which she prayed, "My dear Mother, I ask you pardon for all the pain I have caused you by my infidelities in the religious life, and I also ask pardon of my companions for the many bad examples I have given them... especially for my pride!". In those last weeks the psychological torments gave way to lucidity, despite the continuing physical pain. By Easter of 1879 her life was drawing to a close. On Wednesday 16th April Sister Marie-Bernard could no longer tolerate lying in bed. She was moved to a nearby armchair. The Sisters gave her a crucifix which she kissed and gazed at with love. In response to the Sisters reciting the Hail Mary she said, "Holy Mary, Mother of God, pray for me, a poor sinner, a poor sinner...". After making the sign of the Cross she was then given a sip from a glass of cordial. Her head then sank forward, and this faithful, suffering servant offered her soul to the Lord.

In doing so, she fulfilled the promise that she made to Pope Pius IX in her letter to him:

"My weapons are prayer and sacrifice,
and I will keep them until my last breath.
Then, finally, the weapon of suffering
will fall from my hand.
But the weapon of prayer will follow me to heaven,
where it will be even more powerful."

SAINT BERNADETTE
AND THE MESSAGES OF LOURDES

Bernadette's funeral was held on 19th April 1879, having been delayed a day to cater for those large numbers who wished to pay final homage to her. After the funeral the coffin was removed to a chapel in the Convent. In death, as in life, consideration had to be given as to how her privacy was to be protected; it was decided that she would not join her fellow Sisters in the public graveyard but would be interred in a specially constructed crypt. This happened on 22nd May 1879. There was, of course, immediate speculation as to when her canonisation process would start, as she was almost considered to be a saint in her own lifetime. However, the Church has always maintained prudence in affairs such as this, and in order to consider from the perspective of elapsed time and allow any transient sentiment and contemporary enthusiasm to die down, as well as objectively assess the fruits of her life and after, it was not until 1909 that the Vatican initiated the *Procès Ordinaire* to examine the case for Beatification. Exhumation of the body is part of this process, and in September of that year, her body was found to be incorrupt, a witness noting that it was, "completely intact, without odour, almost mummified".

Canonisation process

There were two further exhumations in the process leading up to her canonisation, the final one being during 1925 at the time of the final enquiry (*Procès Apostolique*), where although there were some changes to the body, it was still in an incorrupt state. Whilst the Church makes no claim of the miraculous over instances of incorruption, it is nonetheless obvious, according to one expert commentator, that in Bernadette's case, for whatever reason, "she benefited from a fairly rare biological phenomenon".

On 14th June 1925 Bernadette was beatified, giving her the title 'Blessed' and approval for her veneration. She was canonised by Pope Pius XI eight years later on 8th December 1933. In the Canon of Saints she is formally listed as Saint Marie-Bernard, but to everybody, she is still that young, resolute peasant girl from Lourdes - Bernadette. Her feast is celebrated on 16th April. Her body lies in her shrine in the chapel at the Convent of the Sisters of Nevers, her final home and resting place on earth, where, ironically, the curious still come and seek her out, but where also the faithful come to venerate and seek intercession.

Whilst many assumed that later on in her life and at the time of her death Bernadette was a saint, this could not have been a foregone conclusion in the eyes of the Vatican, who in their *Procès* would minutely scrutinise every aspect, good or bad, verbal, or written, not sparing

any detail of her life. Through this process it was evident
that in her life she bore many trials, and had to bear them
under intense, continuous and critical scrutiny. Under this
sort of pressure she never seemed to lose, no doubt
through her heroic efforts and great received grace, her
equilibrium or equanimity to any critical degree.

Trials of a Saint

Amongst, what could be regarded as her more minor
trials, were:

- The attention she had to endure whilst still living at
Lourdes, robustly countered by her consistency and
fidelity to the Apparitions, and her dogged insistence not
to profit materially from her experience.
- The family circumstances of her struggling parents and
siblings - struggling with life, and death, which she bolstered
by her continual encouragement, love and prayers.
- The radical - but entirely voluntary - uprooting of her
life, which could alternatively have been one of fame and
comfort, from Lourdes and her family, and having to
adapt and accept willingly not only the rigours of
religious life, but having to cross quite unfamiliar cultural
and social barriers. This she did with a singular
determination in the firm belief that it was God's will.
- her seemingly never-ending 'inquisition by visitors'
which took a heavy toll on her health and patience, but

which she bore with fortitude and dutiful resignation, although it tested her patience and temper.

- The harshness of her superiors which she bore with humility, but also proved a test for her pride, a fault that she knew she would have to continually struggle with, "I have been rightly told that it will die fifteen minutes after I do", she once wryly commented to a friend.

- Inactivity, something which she hated, and attempted to combat by keeping active, if only embroidering or counselling novices whilst on her sick bed.

Her major trial, without a doubt was her ill-health, which in her final years was incapacitating, prolonged and agonising. All the evidence is there that this is something which she bore with particular acquiescence and fortitude, accepting that, "Our Lord gives His crown of thorns to his friends", and thus willingly translating her illness as her 'job'. This suffering was the Cross quite explicitly given to Bernadette, and how she carried it is the example and inspiration that she gives to those tens of thousands of the sick and disabled who visit Lourdes every year - this heroism was Bernadette's personal and enduring gift to her beloved Lourdes. This gift is beautifully summarised by Father Febvre, her confessor at Nevers, "Her habitual state of suffering would reveal to souls the pathway and the necessity of suffering for those who wished to be, 'happy not in this world but the other'."

The Messages of Our Lady of Lourdes

There were not many words spoken for 'public consumption' by Our Lady when she appeared to Bernadette; of her secrets to Bernadette, we of course, will never know length and content. But the messages that Our Lady imparted for us, whether by word, symbol or implication, are many and multi-layered, giving a wealth to ponder over. They are gentle, reassuring, encouraging, albeit at times woven through with sorrow.

- Firstly, it is significant that Mary, the most elevated of humanity, was sent by God as His messenger to one of the poorest, most obscure and disregarded of humanity. The simple message being that God is accessible to all, welcomes all, and speaks to all, and, conversely, it is often the poorest and most obscure who hear the message and unashamedly transmit it. "How blessed are you who are poor: the kingdom of God is yours" (*Lk* 6:20). One only has to look at Blessed Teresa of Calcutta to see this aspect.

- Next, Our Lady's first words to Bernadette, "What I have to say to you does not have to be written down", is an eloquent statement on Faith - in an age of increasing rationalism and cynicism over the supernatural - tangible and visible 'proof' is not always going to be on hand, "Only faith can guarantee the blessings that we hope for, or prove the existence of realities that are unseen" (*Heb* 11:1).

- In that same third Apparition, the next statement Our
Lady made was, "Would you be kind enough to come here
every day for fifteen days?". This is God's invitation to us
all in its broadest sense, always graciously put, for us to
engage with Him, with the same commitment and
determination, against the opposition, no matter how subtle,
that Bernadette had to face and successfully overcome.
"The promise that was made is for you and your children,
and for all those who are far away, for all those whom the
Lord our God is calling to himself" (*Ac* 2:39). It could also
be taken as an explicit invitation for any one to make the
pilgrimage to Lourdes either for healing or to assist.

- The last remark during that Apparition, that would
not only resonate with Bernadette for the rest of her life,
but should with us too, "I do not promise to make you
happy in this world, but in the other", is God's sure
promise to us, His broken and struggling people in this
'vale of tears', that, through our honest endeavour to
follow His will, and despite the hardships of this world,
we will find eternal peace and happiness with Him in the
other. "In my estimation, all that we suffer in the present
time is nothing in comparison with the glory which is
destined to be disclosed for us, for the whole creation is
waiting with eagerness for the children of God to be
revealed" (*Rom* 8:18, 19).

- From the eighth to the twelfth Apparitions the theme
is repentance, where Bernadette's actions - crawling on

her knees, kissing the ground, drinking and washing of the muddy residue from the nascent spring, eating the saxifrage herb, all signify deep acts of penitence, a common theme from many of Our Lady's messages, a theme usually spelt out with a dramatic urgency, coupled with a strong call for conversion. "The time is fulfilled, and the kingdom of God is close at hand. Repent and believe the gospel" (*Mk* 1:15).

- There is, though, a sign of hope in amongst this theme of repentance: the uncovering of the spring indicated by Our Lady. This is the 'living water', "the water that I shall give will well up in them and will become a source of eternal life" (*Jn* 4:14), and in the particular context of Lourdes, the healing water.

- The calls, in the thirteenth and fourteenth Apparitions, to bring people in procession and build a chapel has even more poignancy and relevance today: processions are rarely seen, chapels and churches are closing down in many parts of the world, but Lourdes remains a faithful rallying point to this call. "So, since God has chosen you to build a house for his sanctuary, go resolutely to work!" (*1 Ch* 28:10). The reference to 'build a chapel' does not only refer to bricks and mortar, but also to people, "Now Christ's body is yourselves, each of you with a part to play in the whole" (*1 Co* 12:27).

- That of the sixteenth Apparition, "I am the Immaculate Conception" was the one that astounded the

Catholic world. Not, "I was immaculately conceived", but, "I AM the Immaculate Conception", signifying a resounding confirmation by God, through Our Lady, to the declaration of the dogma of the Immaculate Conception four years earlier by Pope Pius IX, and an unequivocal endorsement of Papal infallibility.

Poverty, Penance, Prayer

When René Laurentin, a distinguished Marian scholar, collated and analysed the chance words of Bernadette, he, "was greatly surprised that they almost grouped themselves under the key words of the message of Lourdes: poverty, penance, prayer". And these are the overarching components of Our Lady's message from Lourdes, and indeed the Christian message. Bernadette most certainly reflected these attributes throughout her life, Our Lady entreats us all to do the same. Poverty is that attitude that God seeks most from us, as preached by Jesus in the Beatitudes; penance is the continual actions we take in acknowledging our weaknesses, repairing them and thereby returning as soon as we can back to God's love; prayer is seeking that intimate dialogue with God, not necessarily only through words or song, but also through our intentions and our actions. All three should be bound in that inestimable element of the Almighty: Love.

THE LOURDES MIRACLES

John Traynor

"Out in the open now I ran towards the Grotto, which is about two or three hundred yards from the Asile. This stretch of ground was gravel then, not paved, and I was barefoot. I ran the whole way to the Grotto without getting the least mark or cut on my bare feet. The *brancardiers* were running after me but they could not catch up with me. When they reached the Grotto, there I was on my knees, still in my night clothes, praying to Our Lady and thanking her." What is remarkable about this story is not the undamaged bare feet or the outrunning of the *brancardiers,* but the fact that the afternoon before, John Traynor had been a partly paralysed epileptic who had not walked for eight years.

His condition was a result of war wounds from World War I. Subsequent operations to join severed nerves in his useless arm were unsuccessful, and he had a steel plate inserted in his skull to protect his exposed brain and to ameliorate the epilepsy - which it had not. He was wheelchair bound, doubly incontinent and certified as being permanently and completely disabled by the War Pensions Agency, being awarded a 100% disability pension.

Pilgrims gathering at the Grotto - Lourdes.

He was cured as he was being blessed by Jesus in the Blessed Sacrament whilst on pilgrimage to Lourdes in July 1923. He is one of the many thousands of cures that have come out of Lourdes. His cure can openly be discussed as inexplicable because it was examined by the Medical Bureau at Lourdes who concluded in their official report on 6th October 1926, "this extraordinary cure is absolutely beyond and above the powers of nature". The doctors who examined him could find no trace of paralysis or epilepsy, his previously atrophied arm and shoulder muscles were fully restored, the hole in his skull had fused over with bone - there was no trace of the steel plate, and he was fully mobile again.

Curiously, despite this evidence, his case never went forward for the process of canonical acceptance and registration as an 'official' miracle, although in the words of the Bureau's account of this case, "there was no doubt about the evidence for a miracle in people's minds". He died of non-related causes more than twenty years later, having subsequently worked as and run a coal merchants business for most of it. As for the officials at the War Pensions, they could not (or would not) accept this cure, and for the rest of his life he remained officially 'incapacitated'!

Miraculous cures

Although it has been stated that thousands of cures have come out of Lourdes, there are, in fact, only sixty six to date that have been officially accepted or authenticated by the Church as miraculous, or put in more modern terms, 'a personal gift of God' to an individual. The reason for this small number is due to the thorough and painstaking investigations that are required of the claimed cure, accompanied by the unequivocal prior evidence that is needed to support it on the medical side. This process, involving four distinct stages, has evolved over time and experience since the first cures were claimed in 1858. Just as important as it is to authenticate cures, is its role in detecting fraudulent claims, of which there have been instances from those who wish to discredit Lourdes or even the Gospel message of miracles.

Authentication

The first three stages of authentication all involve painstaking medical and clinical investigation, moving from initial investigation at the Lourdes Medical Bureau, up through the International Medical Association of Lourdes, which is made up from doctors with the necessary clinical and pathological skills, regardless of faith or belief. Any bias towards the Church, or indeed any desire for a wishful outcome, is further avoided by the Association being financially independent. If the case warrants, it will move on to the last medical stage of being examined by the Lourdes International Medical Committee, established in 1947, and consisting of up to twenty medical specialists competent to scrutinise in depth the nature of the original condition and the cure. This aspect of the activities of Lourdes was emphasised by Pope John Paul II when in November 1988 he reminded the medical personnel there that the verification of miraculous cures is Lourdes' "special responsibility and mission".

In broad terms the criteria that they will work with is that established by Prospero Lambertini (the future Pope Benedict XIV) in 1743, for authenticating miracles attributed to candidates for beatification or canonisation. These include: the medical condition being considered as incurable, no treatment or medication having been given which could possibly have contributed to or effected any cure, the cure must be sudden and complete with no relapse. Within those parameters, "a passage from an established pathological state to a state of health" must be fully demonstrated. In human terms, an occurrence that is 'inexplicable'

Having successfully accomplished the third stage, the case may then be passed to the claimant's diocesan bishop who, in forming a canonical committee, will consider all aspects of the case, including the person's disposition and religious attitude, the fruits that have flowed from it, and its fidelity to the Gospel, before declaring it to be of miraculous nature to the Church and the world.

Many other cures

Over the last hundred years it is estimated that in excess of 6,500 claimed cures have been registered at the Medical Bureau. Of these, at least 2,500 have been considered as incredible, but lacked the necessary depth of evidence or agreement to proceed to the next stage. According to the present Director of the Medical Bureau, about thirty five to forty cases a year currently pass through the Bureau that warrant further investigation; at the time of writing there are two cases under consideration for going through the full process to canonical investigation.

The most recent of the authenticated miracles was that of Frenchman Jean-Pierre Bely in February 1999, who having been diagnosed with Multiple Sclerosis in 1984, was taken to Lourdes in 1987, completely paralysed and bedridden, and, "in a sudden, unexpected and unforeseen way regained his normal functions". In accepting this cure as miraculous, his Bishop, Monsignor Claude Dagens, invited, "all the faithful to thank God for this healing, and all the ill to be the witness of this faith among us, not resigning to their disease, but wishing the advent of the new Creation, at last relieved of illness, of sin and of death".

'A place of healing for all'

Of course, it is these high profile and incredible healings that tend to dominate and give the impression that it is only on this scale that healing occurs at Lourdes. But it is plainly evident that there are, even when just listening to simple anecdotal accounts, countless other personal miracles happening daily at every sort of level and dimension, where minds and spirits have been healed in many manifestations, where conversion, re-orientation and a return to the Faith have occurred. In some cases of serious illness or condition of life, where, although healing has not occurred, a deep peace and the grace of acceptance has been granted instead.

And really this is what Lourdes is about, a place of healing for all, from the high-profile, to the gentle, sometimes intangible cure of minds, bodies and spirits. Healings that anyway would be impossible to examine objectively, assuming that those who experienced it would have wished to submit it to scrutiny in the first place. In the words of Father Michael Beattie SJ, a seasoned worker-visitor to Lourdes, "Any priest who is called upon to exercise his priestly ministry in this place will abundantly testify to this. People, both sick and able-bodied, come to Lourdes and go home again having 'found their feet!'"

Doctor Bernard Colvin, a member of the International Medical Committee and orthopaedic surgeon at the Royal Infirmary Hospital in Dundee commented that many miracles may have been missed through lack of complete evidence or the modern rigours of examination. He went on, "But a miracle doesn't have to be labelled by one of us for it to be true. Its really between God and the patient". And at whatever level that miracles are recognised - whether by the Church to wide public acclaim and thanksgiving, to the joyful but private realisation of an individual acknowledging healing in the privacy of their own heart - can be linked to the thought of Doctor Patrick Thellier, the current Medical Director of the Sanctuary, that in needing to recognise that miracles still exist today is, "to recognise that Christ is the only doctor that can be a source of healing for all of us", and that Lourdes, "by the divine mercy of God is a place of healing for all".

LOURDES AND PILGRIMAGE TODAY

The Lourdes of today could be summed up as 'a tale of three towns'. At its heart is the Domain, or Sanctuary, some 52 hectares of beautifully kept and cared for grounds and buildings, in which the principal pilgrim activities and liturgical venues of Lourdes are located. Immediately outside and surrounding the Domain is the commercial 'engine' of Lourdes, shop upon shop selling religious artefacts for every taste, and phalanxes of hotels, cafes and restaurants, many overlooking the River Gave. Lourdes boasts more hotels, outside Paris, than any other place in France. And lastly, fringing these areas, are those parts of the town which would be indistinguishable from any other French provincial town. The grey-green River Gave still rushes through, the old military fort dominates from above, and the lush, green foothills of the Pyrénées look down on the town, just as in Bernadette's days.

Each of these areas have their own atmosphere. The Sanctuary, which saw an estimated six million pilgrims in 2002, has thousands circulating through it every day, and at times it can seem thronging and busy in places, but there is nonetheless a predominant air of calm and dignity. Despite the crowds, there is also the impression of space, and the whole place is structured to accommodate pilgrims comfortably, whether it be in a quiet corner singly or in small groups, or for the huge gatherings for the main liturgical events of the day. Outside the Domain, in the commercial area, there is a distinct change of pace and atmosphere: it is crowded and bustling, narrow streets, shops and cafes spilling out into the pavements, many people good naturedly on the move.

Throughout, there is of course a noticeable presence of the sick, infirm and disabled, and the ethos of Lourdes is such that wherever they are, they are given the VIP treatment. This was evident, with wheelchairs and 'chariots' having their own priority routes through the Domain, and being given preference of passage in the town. Pedestrians and traffic seemed to mix quite amicably, although motorists whose visit straddles the 1st or 16th of each month should be aware that the one-way system reverses itself on these dates in order to give shopkeepers an equal trading advantage throughout the month!

The Domain

On entering the Domain at the main St Michael's Gate, one's eye is immediately drawn from the striking Breton Calvary tableau at the entrance, down the wide, flag bedecked, tree lined boulevard, straight to the spires, domes, ramparts, arches and glittering gold crown of the Basilicas of Lourdes. On walking down this boulevard one notices to the left a very large, grassed oval mound, which one only discovers later to be the 'roof' of the underground Basilica of St Pius X. Built between 1956 and 1958 in a stark and modern style for the centenary of the Apparitions, it is nonetheless an impressive structure of 12,000m^2 depicting an upturned boat under which one shelters, 'the barque of St Peter', and capable of holding up to 20,000 pilgrims for major liturgical events. Having got to the end of the boulevard one is greeted by the Crowned Statue of Our Lady, presiding gracefully over the main square by the Basilicas, Rosary Square, another major gathering place for pilgrim worship. When one starts to explore the Basilicas it is apparent that what initially appeared to be one building is in fact three quite separate churches.

Basilica Churches

Of these, the Crypt was the first to be built as the direct response to Our Lady's, "Go tell the priests to have a chapel built here". It was placed directly above the Grotto. Bernadette's father, François, was part of the work-force digging the excavations. It was opened in May 1866, eight short years after the Apparitions, on the Vigil of Pentecost by the Bishop of Tarbes, with Bernadette present. It is an exquisite, small, intimate pillared-and-arched chapel with seating for about 120. Above the altar is a glorious statue of Our Lady within a radiant, golden sun-burst surround. A small side chapel houses relics of St Bernadette. Apart from use as a prayer and Mass venue during the day, Adoration is available in the small hours during the pilgrim season, April to October. Amongst the hundreds of *ex voto* offerings round the chapel (wall plaques with messages of thanks for Our Lady's intercessions) was one with heartfelt thanks for 'helping me pass my exams'; it seems that no matter is too small for Our Lady's attentions!

Built above the Crypt is the Upper Basilica, the Basilica of the Immaculate Conception, being blessed and opened in August 1871, and raised to the status of a Minor Basilica in 1874 by Pope Pius IX. This has a more lofty, 'conventional church' feel about it, and can seat 550 pilgrims. Every hour the spire bells peal the Lourdes *'Ave Maria'*. The neo-Byzantine styled Rosary Basilica, with the great gold crown atop the dome, makes up the last of this trio of churches, being built below the Crypt between 1883 and 1889. It is the largest of the three, seating 1500, which at the time of writing was being extensively worked on to repair water ingress damage. Nonetheless one could still appreciate the fine mosaic work of this church, shaped as a Greek cross, depicting the Mysteries of the Rosary in the side chapels.

All three churches are intimately joined, bound together not only by common walls and brickwork, but also by time, and the prayer and worship of those pilgrims inside, as well as those gazing in awe, outside. This unification is physically made complete by the majestic, sweeping ramparts, the lower ones of which arc outwards, as if to embrace Rosary Square, and the pilgrims within it, like two huge welcoming arms.

The Grotto

Wandering on under the arches of the northern ramparts of the Basilicas one quite suddenly and unexpectedly comes upon the Grotto of Massabielle. Recognition is instant, it is exactly as depicted in the many pictures and drawings of Bernadette's time that one has seen prior to visiting. It is an area of intense devotion and attention, with the focus being on the white statue of Our Lady of Lourdes in the crevice above the Grotto. Underneath, the words exactly as they were spoken by Our Lady to Bernadette in the local patois, *'Que soy era Immaculada Councepciou'*. Inside the Grotto a small altar, and in front an ever-burning pyramid of candles. Pilgrims sit, stand or kneel all round in rapt prayer and reflection. At times there is a queue as pilgrims patiently wait to file into the Grotto itself, to look up at the statue and see Our Lady as Bernadette did, to pray or leave their prayer intentions, to wonder at the spring that has flowed so prodigiously since Our Lady instructed Bernadette to uncover it, and as they file through, they give a loving, lingering and pensive caress to the Grotto rock, already worn and polished smooth by the many millions of hands with similar intent over the years.

Just beyond the Grotto are two long rows of metal shuttered stalls in which many hundreds of candles, of many sizes, lovingly and prayerfully placed by pilgrims, unendingly blaze as a constant and visible demonstration of the prayers, hopes, sorrows, joys and petitions of the faithful, ever rising upwards in unceasing prayer.

The Immersion Baths

Beyond the candles, overlooking the Gave, is the area where the immersion baths are located. At first glance it is an unprepossessing looking place, rather like a gloomy, run-down provincial bus terminal. On this impression, and the fact that I hate being immersed in cold water, did not particularly motivate me to partake. But..... "Go drink of the spring and wash yourself there" was the message of Our Lady to Bernadette, and the six men's and eleven women's baths are geared to do just that, as testified by the 380,000 pilgrims who went through in 2002.

The waters, which come from the Grotto spring, have themselves long been a subject of curiosity and study. In the early days it was thought that they may have had some therapeutic content, which, if not brought on, certainly aided, the healing process. Subsequent laboratory analysis showed it to be no more than typical pure spring water filtering down from the mountains, with no detectable therapeutic qualities. A more notable feature of the baths was that they have never posed a serious hazard to health, despite the fact that in the early years the water was only changed twice a day, and the sick and diseased were bathed one after the other, some with suppurating wounds and septic sores. Nowadays, it is regularly circulated and sterilised.

So, despite my reservations and my pride I entered the baths area. It was immediately apparent that something very special was going on here, despite the stark surroundings; this feeling was engendered straight away by the men who operate the baths - they did so throughout with great dignity and reverence, in a gentle, respectful and prayerful manner. You are encouraged to recollect yourself before immersion, and to give thanks afterwards. How the processing and immersion is done I will leave for each pilgrim to experience when their time comes, suffice it to say it was beautiful. Despite my aversion to immersion (the baths are at 12 ºC), I did not experience my usual reaction to a cold dunking, and in fact seemed oblivious to the cold water. The other thing that intrigued me was a remark made by our tour courier beforehand, "You come out dry". The thought of putting clothes on straight after getting out of the bath at home would just not be entertained, but in effect that is what one does after the immersion, and, yes, you do come out 'dry'.

However, all this was trivia compared to the subsequent effect that immersion had on me and for my peace and prayer afterwards - both quite unexpected.

Without even thinking or knowing, I found myself at the Grotto starting to pray, and it was one of those very rare occasions where the prayer was free-flowing, unhindered, and despite the number of people around me, completely undistracted. I felt a very strong personal presence of Our Lady with me, so much so that when I began to think of moving on after some minutes (I had a meeting to go to) I found that I was unable to pick up my day pack to put on my back and (much to my delight) felt this strong and persistent compulsion to stay! It happened a second time, and it was only after another while did I feel a positive consent to go on my way. This was without doubt the highlight of my pilgrimage, and as I am slowly learning, God reveals Himself at quite the most unexpected moments, and in this case, with my reluctance to go to the baths, with an exquisite and wry sense of humour, clearly using my weakness to make a point!

Recently installed opposite the Grotto on the other side of the river is the *Chemin de l'eau,* a row of nine taps and basins, to enable pilgrims to 'wash at the fountain', who for whatever reason, do not wish to enter the baths.

Around the Domain

Around the Domain there are many other places of worship. The Chapel of St Joseph by St Michael's Gate; the very modern, large Church of St Bernadette, placed on the spot across the river where Bernadette knelt during the final Apparition; there is a small Adoration Chapel immediately next door, where Exposition of the Blessed Sacrament takes place from after the afternoon procession up until close to midnight. In the Meadow (or *Prairie*) area there is a larger Adoration tent where the Blessed Sacrament is exposed for most of the day. The large expanse of the Meadow gives plenty of capacity for major celebrations, focussing in on a canopied stage and altar. At other times it also contributes to the sense of space and peace within the Domain.

On one side of the main boulevard, with quite pointedly a statue of the Curé d'Ars outside, is the Chapel of Reconciliation. This building has 48 confessionals and a spacious preparatory area; confessions are heard in most of the major European languages, including English. There are also many other minor chapels and places of worship, inside and out of the Domain, of which details are given in the guide books.

On a wooded hillside, just outside the Domain and overlooking Lourdes, are the Stations of the Cross, winding their way along an undulating 1500 metre path, each Station depicted by dramatic life-size cast iron statues, and skilfully using the natural features of the land. This Way is not suitable for pilgrims in wheelchairs, who are catered for by the alternative Stations of the Cross for the Sick in the Meadow by the bridge beyond the Grotto.

Other features and buildings associated with Lourdes
and Bernadette's life also abound. There are, in the
Domain, the many administrative buildings, meeting and
conference rooms, including the all important Medical
Bureau which processes the claims for miraculous cures.
Outside, the *cachot* is easily accessible up the hill in the
old town, as is Boly Mill, Fr Peyramale's Presbytery (now
the public library) and the Hospice where Bernadette
boarded and completed her education. There are also the
buildings, churches, houses and convents of the forty four
religious communities that live in and around Lourdes; the
Poor Clares Monastery in the middle of town is one which
provides a welcome haven in their peaceful chapel. A
short excursion, or even walk, will take one to Bartres to
see the sheepfold where Bernadette tended her flock, the
Lagues house, and the Parish Church.

In keeping with the Lourdes effort to cater for their
VIPs - the infirm, sick and disabled - there are extensive
facilities for these pilgrims in every aspect of their lives,
from their mobility to their worshipping, to living
accommodation. One of the most visible and striking of
these efforts is the *Accueil Notre-Dame,* a large modern
building just across the Gave, capable of accommodating
943 sick pilgrims at any one time, and with over 29,000
sick pilgrims having passed through in 2002. It is run by
the Sisters of Charity of Nevers, Bernadette's
Congregation. This type of accommodation is described

as 'not a hotel, nor a hospital', but has, nonetheless, all the facilities to cope with the many categories of sick pilgrim. The building provides the necessary accommodation and catering, the pilgrim parties provide the medical expertise, supplies and helpers to look after and care for their sick pilgrims. The other major *Accueil* of this sort in the town is the long established (1877) Marie St Frai, refurbished in 1998, having four hundred beds, and run by the Daughters of Our Lady of Sorrows.

Major Events

Of course, all this extensive infrastructure is there to serve the purpose of helping the pilgrim to glorify God, plead for intercession and seek healing. There are major events during the pilgrim season which facilitate this. Early every evening there is the procession to, and the Blessing of the Sick in, the Pius X Basilica. This is a particularly moving and inspiring event, as one witnesses the quiet, orderly and expectant gathering of the sick and their helpers prior to setting off from the Adoration tent ahead of the Blessed Sacrament, and then the great tide of wheelchairs, stretchers, chariots and pedestrians processing along the boulevard to the accompaniment of prayers and hymns coming from the Basilica. Those inside follow the procession's progress on the large but discreet video screens, the climax being the arrival of the procession and finally the Blessed

Sacrament, followed by a period of praise, worship and Adoration, ending in the Blessing.

The last major event of the day is the candlelit Rosary procession which sets off from the Grotto, along the boulevard and ending in a great gathering in Rosary Square - a vast sea of twinkling lights in the darkness, great waves of prayer and song rising heavenward. On looking down on this impressive gathering from the top rampart, one can only reflect on Our Lady's call, "Tell the priests and people to come here in procession" and realise how effectively and faithfully that call has been answered. One can almost feel Bernadette's continuing amazement and gratitude as to how this remarkable place and gathering of people has come about. Twice a week every Wednesday and Sunday morning is the International Mass, held in the underground Basilica, where one can rejoice in the great gathering of the family of nations. All these events are seasonal, but timings and locations are well publicised.

These large scale, centrally organised devotions cater for the pilgrim community as a whole, but outside of them there continues a whole range of activities and devotions on varying scales throughout the day and night all over the Domain, as the diocesan, parish and other groups and associations, and individuals, carry out their specific devotions and programmes of activity. I came across a large Irish

The Basilica - Lourdes.

diocesan pilgrim group, 600 pilgrims led by their
Bishop, with forty priests, eighty sick and infirm,
doctors and nurses, attendant *brancardiers* and
handmaids, and many young people, all giving of their
time to help and to experience the privilege of a unique
form of humble service. Many groups are identifiable
with their banners and/or distinct uniforms. The
brancardiers are conspicuous with the canvas or
leather harness straps worn over the shoulders, which
were formerly used to help take the weight of a
stretcher, but now more a badge of office in the
running of the Domain, and in organising and tending
to the needs of the sick pilgrims.

The Eucharist

All the foregoing has quite naturally centred round Our
Lady, for, after all, it is her 'Domain'. However, one is
struck by the centrality of the Eucharist at Lourdes - the
Real Presence of her Son, ever-present, constantly
celebrated throughout the day and night. This presence is
manifested in the many Masses that are said throughout
the Domain and Lourdes - whether at one of the major
daily celebrations, or in one of the many smaller churches
and side chapels, such as the *Salles,* off St Bernadette's
church, celebrated by the many visiting priests and
smaller groups. Availability of Eucharistic Adoration is
generous, and the Blessed Sacrament Procession of the

Sick is a visible demonstration of those who follow, adore and hope in Jesus, the Lord; a demonstration by those led there by His loving Mother, Mary.

Volunteers and Organisations

The umbrella organisation for all this volunteer effort is the *Hospitalité de Notre-Dame de Lourdes* which co-ordinates the volunteer effort and helps with the control and the smooth running of the Domain activities. This organisation is supplemented by national or diocesan *Hospitalités,* and many, many other groups of volunteer organisations from many countries with many skills and services to offer, all coping with, in 2002, the 64,000 sick pilgrims that passed through Lourdes. One notable organisation from UK and Ireland is HCPT, the Handicapped Children's Pilgrimage Trust, which brings thousands of handicapped children, and their 'helpers' to Lourdes each year. Without the many other organisations involved the overall human 'miracle' of Lourdes would just not occur. Further details will be found at the official Lourdes website (see Bibliography).

The young and the poor

As well as catering for the sick, Lourdes also concentrates on Youth, which is highly appropriate when one thinks of the age of the young seer who delivered Our Lady's messages and inspired the Lourdes phenomenon.

In organisational terms there is a Youth Service geared up to welcome and assist young pilgrims as they pass through, a youth village which accommodated over 17,000 young people in 2002, and a residential School of Evangelisation for young people aged between 20 and 25.

The poor have not been overlooked either. A short distance from Lourdes is the *Cité Saint-Pierre,* an accommodation and conference complex, run by *Secours Catholique/Caritas France,* that can house 500 pilgrims at any one time, having accepted over 20,000 poor and destitute pilgrims in 2002. Its purpose is "to give place and voice to the most insignificant and to the rejected in a pilgrimage". It also depends on a huge volunteer effort from those willing to give three weeks of their time. Further details can be obtained, as with many other organisations, through the Lourdes website (see Bibliography) or through dioceses.

There are two *Cenacolos,* inspirational establishments run by and for recovering addicts; one in Lourdes, catering for up to sixty young men, and the other in *Adé* some 4 kilometres outside, for up to 30 young women; visitors are welcome.

Healing and Hope

Lourdes is not about the story of a poor peasant girl, the wondrous things she experienced, and the town she lived in. The story and subsequent events are just one of many ways in which God's message of salvation is conveyed to the world. In this case a message of Healing and Hope. Many who know about Lourdes immediately associate it with the very sick and their miraculous healing, this aspect is but God's eye-catching 'advertisement' for the Lourdes message. Because underneath these high profile cases lie the millions of other miracles, large and small, that have happened to those drawn, for whatever reason, to go there, even to those who seek the intercession of St Bernadette and Our Lady of Lourdes from afar. They may have considered themselves able-bodied and healthy, but they may have not realised their own spiritual or other malaise. The experience of Lourdes may reveal that, and the healing, or conversion process by God's grace, gets under way. God's Healing is there for all. We do not even have to wait for Jesus to say, "Stretch out your hand" (*Lk* 6:10), we just have to offer it - to be healed.

Underlying all this is the ultimate message of Hope. Our Lady did not promise to make Bernadette 'happy in this world', nor us, as we struggle to faithfully follow the Way. In this context we are, "the people who have been through the great trial" (*Rev* 7:14); but the promise, as of that to Bernadette, is that our happiness will be 'in the other', where we will never hunger or thirst again; sun and scorching wind will never plague us, because the Lamb who is at the heart of the throne will be our shepherd and will guide us to springs of living water; and God will wipe away all tears from our eyes (cf *Rev* 7:16, 17).

SELECT BIBLIOGRAPHY

Official Guide of the Sanctuary. Sanctuaires Notre-Dame de Lourdes, 2003.

Sanctuary of Our Lady of Lourdes. Introduction, 2003. Communications Department of the Sanctuary, Lourdes, February 2003.

BROWN, RAYMOND E, ET AL (edited by). *The New Jerome Biblical Commentary*. Geoffrey Chapman, London 2000.

FRANCISCAN FRIARS OF THE IMMACULATE. *Marian Shrines of France*. Academy of the Immaculate. New Bedford, MA, USA. 1998.

JOHNSON, VERNON MGR. *Christian Suffering and Bernadette of Lourdes*. Catholic Truth Society. London. 1997.

LANE J I REV. *The Story of Bernadette*. Catholic Truth Society. London 1997.

LAURENTIN, RENE. *Bernadette of Lourdes*. Darton, Longman, Todd. London, 2001.

LEWIS, C S. *Miracles*. HarperCollins. London 2002.

METZGER, BRUCE M. (edited by). *Oxford Companion to the Bible*. OUP. Oxford 1993.

MORRELL, DAVID PROF. *Medical Aspects of Lourdes*. Private publication produced for Tangney Tours.

TAYLOR, THERESE. *Bernadette of Lourdes*. Burns & Oattes. London. 2003.

THEILLIER, PATRICK DR. *The Vocation of the Medical Bureau*. International Medical Association of Lourdes. France, 1998.

INTERNET: Lourdes Portal Site - *www.lourdes-france.com*